Oliver's Story

"The little owl who did things his way"

Written by Annette M King

Photos by C. Greg Silva
And Annette M King

This is a true story from a little mission to help
wildlife called 'Wild Heart Ranch'.
Enjoy this "Wild Child" Tale!

This book belongs to

_____

Given by

_____

Because I think you are_____!

Date_____

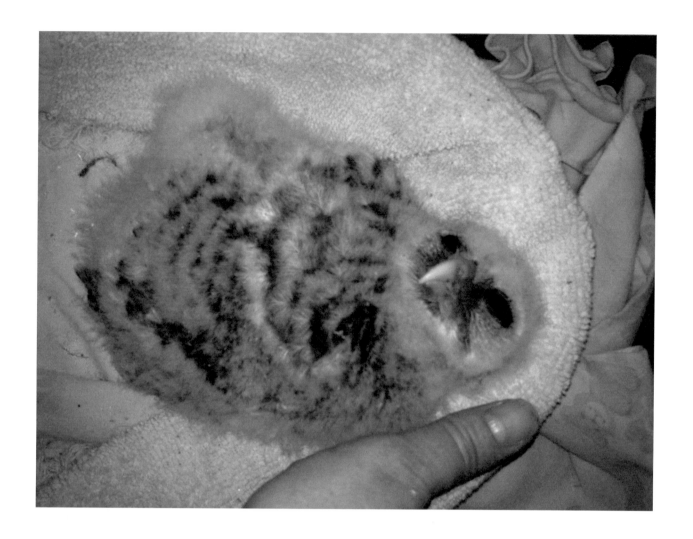

Such a tiny baby barred owl who came in that day many years ago, to a wildlife rescue clinic where we help wild animals who are orphaned or hurt. This owl had lost his mom and had become hungry and cold. Someone found him and brought him right to us. We warmed him and fed him and hoped he would become strong again. I named him Oliver. He needed a name. I could tell the little owl was special.

A few days later, after lots of care, Oliver was feeling much better. He was sitting up in his nest we made for him, waiting for what would come next in his new world with people.

The animals who come here are usually afraid of us at first, but not Oliver. He knew that he needed help and he was so glad we saved him. He was never afraid, not one little bit. Oliver was a brave little owl. He eagerly took the bites of meat we fed him from the tweezers. He wanted to live!

One day another barred owlet arrived. When we put Oliver in with the new owl, he seemed to be telling him that it was okay and not to be afraid. He was happy because he had made a new friend, but his friend had been found as a tiny baby and fed the wrong food for many days before he was brought to us. His legs did not grow properly and the bones were like rubber. The baby was very sick and could not stand and Oliver stayed by his side to comfort him.

Oliver understood his friend had problems and he was very careful around him. He was such a smart little owl and seemed to know that we were trying to help. He always watched us closely and was never afraid. We worked so hard to save his friend, but sadly, it was too late. The little owl could not be saved. It was a very sad day for us and for Oliver. Again, he was alone.

We knew Oliver missed his friend. He was sad and it showed. We struggled to get him eating again and it took days to get him back on track. Oliver was a sensitive baby and seemed to understand that he was alone in the world but for us. It wasn't enough. He knew he was different. It took many days of force feeding him to make sure he got food, but he didn't like having his beak pried open and food pushed into his mouth. It just broke our hearts to upset him. Oliver was stubborn and when he didn't want to do something, he just wouldn't cooperate.

Eventually Oliver calmed down and started taking food from us again. He was growing fast. Soon his feathers were coming in and he was ready for a cage. It was time to graduate from the baby nest. We were all worried about how he would react. He was such an emotional little fellow and we knew that if he didn't like something, he would just stop eating for us. We moved him to the baby cage and watched him closely. At first everything seemed fine.

Suddenly Oliver stopped eating. He had lots of soft comfy things to cuddle in, but once again Oliver wasn't happy. We knew he still missed his friend but we had to figure out how to cheer him up.
We wished he could tell us what was wrong. We were so worried about him. Oh if only I could understand baby owl talk!

We tried offering Oliver other kinds of meat, we tried stuffed toys and soft comfy blankets and even tried holding him to feed him. Nothing worked. Oliver was unhappy and now we were force feeding him again. We had to figure this out and fix his problem before it was too late.

He just sat in his cage looking at us, needing something to be okay in the world, but we had no idea what it was.

Then one day while we were cleaning his cage, we turned our back and "POOF!" went Oliver out of his cage and onto the table. We let him stay out for a while and Oliver seemed happier. Maybe he wanted out. Could that be it? We offered him bites of meat from the tongs and he took it with no problem! We were so happy that our owl was eating again!

Oliver lay down and took a nap. He was happy to be out of his cage. He was not afraid and he did not feel lost. He just wanted to be free to do things his way.

We soon learned that Oliver would not eat in his cage. He would only eat if he was free. What a little brat! He had control now and he knew it. We couldn't let our baby owl go hungry so we let him out of his cage in the morning and he lived on top of the other cages on the table all day long and gladly ate his food.

Oliver grew and grew. The little owl was no longer so little. He still spent the day out of his cage and was put up at night. He ate very well and he stayed in his spot and never gave us any reason to worry about him.

And then suddenly, one day he was in his spot and I went to care for other animals, and he was GONE! We searched and searched for hours and could not find him! I was frantic! Where has Oliver gone? "Where is Oliver? Where is Oliver? I must find him!" I said.

Oliver had learned to fly that day. He flew from his spot on the cages and found a comfy nest on the shelves of blankets for the animals. What a smart little owl and what a great hiding place! This became the new routine. Oliver might stay on his spot near his cage or he might pick another place to sleep.

As Oliver grew stronger, the places he chose to perch became higher. We tried to keep an eye on him when he was free in the clinic, but somehow he seemed to know when our backs were turned and that is when he would choose his next spot.

Every day, all day long was a game of hide and seek with the young owl. We made a game of it. Instead of playing "Where's Waldo", we played "Where's Oliver". So many good places to hide, but he always liked to nap on the towels and blankets we used for the animals.

When it was time for him to eat, we couldn't reach him to feed him so we had to get him down.

We grabbed the towels he was standing on...

But Oliver knew how to use his new wings! The laundry came tumbling down and...

Oliver kept his spot! Now we had a new challenge! An owl that wouldn't eat in his cage, but we couldn't catch him to feed him. This was not going to be easy! We would have to figure out how to let him have his way and keep him healthy and fed. And we did.

We hand fed Oliver twice a day. Before he came out of his cage we fed him. When we put him up at night we fed him. He still would not eat on his own in the cage and he wouldn't come to us when he was free to eat. Oliver was a lot of work and worry, but he was worth it every day. Every morning I would find him in his cage, ready to eat but even more ready to be OUT! He knew he was an owl and owls do not belong in a cage. I respected his independence and loved him more for it.

Oliver was flying well now but he was still a baby and had to be watched closely, but his adventures in the clinic made for some interesting games of 'hide and seek' when it was time to put him up for the night. Sometimes we searched for hours for him. Other times we found him in the strangest places. It seemed like every day Oliver found a new place to hang out and watch us all working to care for the animals in our clinic.

Some days Oliver guarded the trash and laundry cans...

Some days he played 'King of the dishes"!

Some days we couldn't even use the bathroom alone!

The storage area was a favorite place to hide and spend the day.

And forget washing your hands when Oliver took over the sink! He chose his spot and we just had to work around him. He was independent and in charge of himself. We were just here to serve him.

High up near the ceiling of the fawn room, Oliver watched us feed the baby deer. He was fascinated by them! We never knew what went through his little feathered head, but he was always watching, always thinking, always figuring out the world in our clinic with his adventures.

He was flying strong and it was time to move him to an outside cage and get him ready for release back into the wild. It was a day we were all worried about. Another cage, but this cage would hold him all day and all night. Would our owl eat? We did not know, but it was time for our owl to learn to be an owl.

We prepared a small outside cage so that if we needed to hand feed him we could catch him to do so. Oliver was never tame. We never bonded with him or made him into a pet. He was always a wild animal who belonged to himself. Giving him his freedom in the clinic was something we normally would never do, but it was the only way he was happy in our care.

Moving day came and Oliver was now outside in his new cage and he was once again unhappy. He ignored his food. Day after day his food was untouched and again we were catching him and force feeding him. Our beautiful little owl was depressed. We knew what the problem was but we were not sure if it would be safe to fix it. He couldn't live in the clinic forever.

We decided to take a chance and set him free long before he was ready to be on his own. It would only work if Oliver stayed near the clinic so we could put food out for him. We all crossed our fingers and Greg tossed him up into the air near his cage to see what he would do.

Once again Oliver would be free to do what he wanted, but without the safety of the clinic I was afraid. He flew away from us on perfect wings. Up and away he went as our hearts pounded with the possibility of never seeing our little Oliver again if he flew out of sight. I held my breath, I gritted my teeth, I wrung my hands and as the cameras flashed around me I was afraid I would never see our baby Oliver again!

But Oliver didn't go far. He landed in a tree over our heads and kept his eye on the people who cared for him. I breathed a sigh of relief. He was still a young owl and not quite ready to be on his own and he knew it, but we needed him to learn to take care of himself and eat on his own. We hoped Oliver would cooperate and stay nearby so we could care for him.

Oliver watched everything and everyone from his perch in the trees. He explored the branches and tested his skills flying and landing, even chasing bugs and eating them! Oliver was already learning to hunt!

Oliver was even trying to eat the leaves on the trees! He was absolutely willing to eat. Now our challenge was to show him his food pan and hope he would fly down to it and eat on his own. It was the only way our plan would work.

    Of course my brilliant little owl figured everything out! This is Oliver waiting for us to bring him his breakfast. He would be on the deck railing every morning and every night and spend the day in the trees around the clinic. Oliver was always watching us feed and care for the animals just as he had always done inside, but now he was truly free to act like a proper owl. He did things his way as always. He was in charge of how we helped him. What a funny little owl he was!

Oliver ate on his own every day for several weeks. He was also learning to find food. He visited less and less until finally, he no longer needed our support. He had once again figured things out his way, but now he was a grown owl living his life free. He could go wherever he wanted when he wanted. He was beautiful and strong. He visited us a few times to let us see how well he was doing. He ignored the food we offered him and avoided us completely from high in the trees. Eventually Oliver left our lives forever, now completely on his own. Mission accomplished! We had finally done it! (His way!)

HIGH FOUR!!!!

About the author;

I founded Wild Heart Ranch many years ago after someone handed over a pair of orphaned raccoons who had nowhere to go for help. Today, I have cared for more than 40,000 wild animals. This is a photo of me exercising a bald eagle who had recovered from an injury and was preparing for release. I always love them enough to let them go and be who they were born to be. They are never 'mine'. Wild animals always and only belong to themselves.

-Annette

Made in the USA
Columbia, SC
23 November 2024

46766433R00022